# Aches & Pains

# ACHES & PAINS

# MAEVE BINCHY

## Illustrations by
## Wendy Shea

**DELACORTE PRESS**

Published by
Delacorte Press
Random House, Inc.
1540 Broadway
New York, New York 10036

First published in Ireland in 1999.

Delacorte Press® is a registered trademark of Random House, Inc., and the
colophon is a trademark of Random House, Inc.

Library of Congress Cataloging in Publication Data
Binchy, Maeve.
Aches & pains / Maeve Binchy ; illustrations by Wendy Shea.
p. cm.
ISBN 0-385-33510-5
1. Hospital care—Humor. 2. Medicine—Humor. I. Title: Aches & pains.
II. Title.
R705 .B56 2000
362.1'1'0207—dc21
99-087352

BOOK DESIGN BY GLEN M. EDELSTEIN

Manufactured in the United States of America.
Published simultaneously in Canada.

June 2000

RRH   10   9   8   7   6   5   4   3   2   1

For dear Gordon, and all the other good people who made me better.

—MAEVE BINCHY

For Freida and Eileen—there's only one of each of them.

—WENDY SHEA

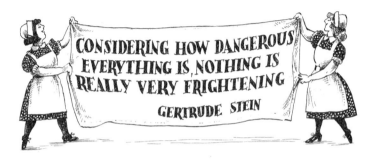

CONSIDERING HOW DANGEROUS EVERYTHING IS, NOTHING IS REALLY VERY FRIGHTENING

GERTRUDE STEIN

# Aches & Pains

# A Note From Maeve

I never knew anyone who went through life without feeling ill at least SOME of the time.

So this is a book that we hope will help you cheer up enormously in all aspects of whatever is wrong!

It happened that my artist friend Wendy Shea and I, who are roughly the same age, had to go to the hospital for hip replacement surgery at roughly the same time. We were in different Dublin hospitals, but phoned each other from time to time to compare notes. What we needed, we told each other, was some reassuring little manual that wouldn't be too taxing to read, but might provide some huge and valuable insights into the whole business of being sick. A nice bossy little book that would tell us to stop feeling sorry for ourselves and yet be fairly sympathetic as well. As we told each other tales of elastic stockings that would not go either up or down the leg, of visitors who stayed for hours, of people who told us about their symptoms when we only wanted to talk about ours, we realized that we were desperate for this "cheer up" book.

So, being Irish and therefore of the temperament that believes nothing is impossible . . . we decided to write it ourselves. Our friends said it was a passing phase, that once we were cured we would forget it all—Wendy would go back to her painting and drawing, I would go back to writing novels. But we had much more moral fiber than anyone believed. We sat down and did it. And now here it is for you to examine!

So, with the confidence of survivors, we are telling you in words and pictures what it was like for us.

And I will begin, as all patients love to do, with MY OWN STORY.

I spent years of my life hiding the fact that I was lame. Why? Because I foolishly feared that people might think I was over the hill and not give me work anymore, and because I didn't want endless discussion about it or pity.

So how did I hide it? Mainly by being in places much earlier than anyone else so that they didn't see me limp in. If I was meeting people in a café, I would be well-installed before they arrived, and then let them leave ahead of me, pretending I had more work to do, or calls to make, before I left so they wouldn't see me limping out.

I used to look at each short journey to be made and work out how many litter bins there were along the street. They are truly great things to sit on, and you can always pretend you are studying a map or reading a paper.

If I was invited to a function in a public place, I'd telephone in advance and ask if I could have a bar stool to sit on. If I was invited to a private house where people were expected to stand, I would ask if they had a kitchen stool and perch myself on it in a nice, handy area where it was possible to talk to everyone. I would ask people to my place rather than go to theirs.

I learned bridge, and then immediately demanded that all my friends learn it, since it was nice and sedentary and no one knew whether you were lame or not.

If ever I was going to stay in a hotel, I would write and say it didn't matter what kind of room it was as long as it was near the lift. In a theater or a movie I would ask for an aisle seat near the back row.

If I hadn't hidden it properly, and on a rare occasion someone insensitively asked me why I was limping, I gave some totally unlikely explanation, like a skiing accident, a fall from a trapeze, or a sexual experiment with a chandelier that had somehow misfired.

It amused nobody but myself really, but no one ever asked again.

Then eventually the thought came, even to a coward like me permanently into denial, that something could be done about this. I had kept hoping that it was like a summer cold, that it might just go away on its own.

But it wasn't happening.

So one day I agreed to put anxiety behind me and consider, just consider, the possibility of surgery.

Now, listen very carefully: If you need a new hip—believe me—NOBODY will ever tell you about it as straight as I will.

No technical jargon. No ludicrous perfectionist advice about keeping fit. Just the facts, explained both simply and graphically.

Hips rot away. I don't know exactly why; sometimes it's congenital, sometimes it's the result of an injury—but either way, when the ball-and-socket joint that sort of sticks your leg to the trunk of your body starts to decay, you feel terrible.

Now, don't let anyone get away with the words "a touch of arthritis." It's much, much worse. It's as if somebody accidentally left a carving knife in your groin and forgot to take it out. And yet somehow to those who don't know how bad it is, it's seen as some vague, rheumaticky sort of ache originating mainly in the mind.

It gets worse. You can't walk, you can't stand, you can't sleep. You are old before your time, and you can't go out into the streets and cry aloud how really bad you feel or they will think you are mad as well as rheumaticky.

So you go to a doctor, who sends you to get X rays, and if they show that your hip is in bits, be pleased rather than upset. That means they can do something about it.

Then you see an orthopedic surgeon, who, if you are lucky, will agree to give you a new hip.

This is the moment where you really and truly need my advice. It's in three simple words. Go for it.

This is an operation with a huge success rate. You will wake up and the pain will not only have gone . . . it will stay gone.

I was the fattest patient the

surgeon had ever met. I was so fat, the doctor refused to do my surgery. He said that even though he could see that my poor hip was in smithereens, he was afraid I would die on the operating table. If I lost the weight, he said, he would reconsider.

I lost the weight. It was really only possible because I had the carrot of a pain-free life dangling in front of me. I then heard the words that I was to come in for the operation.

I was so excited at first that I told everyone. And I was delighted, but of course in the long reaches of the night I wondered if I was mad. Fortunately, there wasn't too much time to brood before I was in there, lying rigid with terror in a hospital bed in my purple nightie.

They sort of go over you the night before an operation to make sure you are a reasonable risk. Everyone is very cheerful and matter-of-fact. And you sign things about knowing what's involved, and naming your next of kin, and then they say good night.

During the night I got this sudden insight. The insight was that I was mad to be getting a new hip— I was fine as I was. So I couldn't sleep, walk, stand, work, think, or enjoy anything, but basically I was fine. I must have exaggerated my symptoms.

"I must go home now," I thought, and crawled out of bed, and found my two walking sticks and my coat.

I had got as far as the door when the nurse came in and guided me firmly back to bed. Lots of people do this, according to the nurse. It's called a "night hallucination." I lay there glumly until the trolley came.

They don't give you a tranquilizer as I had thought, so you go down wide awake. The operating room looked like something from a television series.

I am a person who believes that something should be said on every occasion. "I think I'll leave it all to you," I said to the surgeon, and they all seemed deeply relieved.

I received an epidural injection, the kind that people often have in labor. I was very afraid I would be awake for it all and know what they were doing and try to stop them. But no, completely the reverse. I must have been given some kind of nice, relaxing drug somewhere along the line, because not only did I feel nothing but I didn't know where I was.

I thought I was in a hotel, entertaining this group of people around my couch. I talked nonstop for whatever number of hours it took. I said I was so sorry that I had chosen a place with such heavy building going on, all that drilling and hammering, but added that, on the other hand, you had to be grateful there was so much building going on these days.

I had absolutely no idea that the drilling and hammering were all on my own leg.

Then, they tell me, after a day in Intensive Care—where apparently I wanted to know all the words to "They Can't Take That Away from Me" and sang tunelessly the bits I remembered—I was brought back to my own bed, where I realized that the pain was gone.

7

So you say it couldn't possibly be so easy? It is. Why would I lie to you?

In my own case, I had horrible, weak, rotten bones, so it took me a bit longer to get out of bed than the rest of my ward. But I was never competitive. Eventually, I was able to limp around the corridors with these total strangers, and I had some wonderful conversations with them. Together we would study the hip manual and note that sexual intercourse could be attempted after so many weeks, which was a good topic of conversation at the water cooler with total strangers.

The hip manual also said that after eight weeks we should be able to drive. "That's great," one man said wistfully. "I always wanted to know how to drive but I never had time to learn. It will be a huge advantage to me."

We learned awful things about healthy eating plans, and good posture, and the amount of exercise that normal people are meant to take. And there were some awful things that followed hip surgery:

— . . . like not being allowed to sleep on your side. There was a horrible contraption in the bed to stop you from doing that.

— . . . like the fact that you didn't seem to own your new hip; it was always referred to as "the surgeon's new hip."

— . . . like you had to slide his hip to the side of the bed before standing up, or lay his hip carefully on a strange triangular cushion that was supposed to be a

Never mind the hip – take a look at those biceps!

chair, or position his hip over a high seat on the toilet.

— ... like the really revolting elastic stockings.

— ... like not being allowed to sit up in bed on your own for moving your bum; instead you had to drag yourself up by this extraordinary gadget that hung over the bed and was meant to develop your arm muscles, I suppose. And for those who used it, I suppose it did.

I just snuggled down and read more and more books. Then I was cured and went home.

I am no role model for anyone. I did not do all the horrific exercise they demanded. I just hated the thought of my lungs filling up with all that air and oxygen and everything if it meant I had to walk vigorously every day.

But now I have no pain whatsoever. I can manage stairs and airports and corridors and I have sleep-filled nights. To me this is reward enough to make me advise anyone else to have the operation.

And what attitudes did I want other people to have to my illness? I didn't want people to tell me about other people who had leaped out of bed two days after the operation and walked three miles. I didn't want to hear about people who had complications.

I suppose, like anyone, I wanted to be treated with concern and affection, but as if things were normal, as they had once been and would be again, not so very far in the future.

If that's what you want, how do you get people to treat you like that? The good news is that it's the invalid who calls the shots. All you have to do to avoid sepulchral sympathy, remorseless heartiness, or off-the-wall cures—choose the one that's most maddening to you—is to send out the right vibes.

I hope there is something in this book that will cheer you up. Not too boisterously, as if a manic face were two inches from yours saying menacingly, "You WILL be good-humored, or else." I have met too many professional Pollyannas in my life to think that good humor can be laid onto people very successfully.

And I hope nothing in this book will suggest that it was written and illustrated by two people with a huge history of courage and stoicism. In fact, when either of us is feeling under the weather the next time we may well have to consult ourselves here to recall why we were so overconfident as to produce a manual advising all around us on attitude and behavior.

But it is written with great sympathy, a fairly light heart, and a genuine belief that nothing is quite as bad as it seems at four o'clock in the morning.

# When You Have to Go to the Hospital

# Don't Believe What You Hear

As soon as you mention that you are going to the hospital, it triggers something in other people and forces them to tell you a hospital horror story.

They want to tell you about some dreadful experience, and if you were to believe them, you would think a hospital is staffed by:

- Bad-tempered nurses whose romances are long since over
- Radiography departments where they lose all the X rays
- Nearsighted interns who can't find the veins to draw blood from
- Deaf personnel who never hear you ringing the bell

You're inclined to believe the gloom merchants when they talk about the horrors connected with illness. But why should you? The hospital has worked fine until now. Why should it fall apart the day that you come in?

You will meet fine good people in the hospital. Trust me. They're well trained; they don't flap in an emergency; they don't faint when they see blood. They are mainly in this business because they actually CARE about other people, and there is one sure thing about the nurses—they are not in it for the money.

REMEDIES  AGAINST  FLEAS

**FUMIGATION WITH BRIMSTONE** or the fresh leaves of pennyroyal sewed in a bag and laid on the bed will have the desired effect.

(*The School of Arts* or *Fountain of Knowledge,* Mrs. De Salis, 1890)

It is, in fact, very reassuring to be among professionals who know what is serious and who realize what is only our own imaginations working overtime. They speak soothingly. If you tell them you're frightened and anxious, they won't tell you to pull yourself together and develop a stronger backbone.

Think positive. In hospitals they make you better. That's meant to be—and is—their job. If you go into the hospital full of dire forebodings, then you'll surely find something that might live up to your expectations. Instead you should say very firmly on Day One that no kinder human beings exist on planet Earth than nurses—and in fact, you may want to take one home with you when it's over—and that no more worthy institutions were ever invented than hospitals.

# How to Be Less Nervous

When I was young I used to pretend to be brave because I was big, and big people aren't ever allowed to be afraid. Somehow we were meant to be able to cope single-handedly at the age of seven with the great hound with slavering jaws that I always thought was around the next corner.

I was afraid that if I went to England I might be eaten by a snake because St. Patrick hadn't banished them from there, and I was distinctly worried that I might look up into a tree and see a vision and become a saint and quite possibly a martyr, since the two often went together.

I was afraid of the dark and hated going upstairs because a terrible monster might be lurking in the attic. I was afraid to climb a tree because I might fall; I was afraid whenever I saw the doctor that he might think I needed an injection or vaccination against something. I was terrified that the dentist would get distracted and drill through my head. I watched buses and trucks carefully in case they suddenly left the road and were about to plow into me.

Whenever I saw an ambulance or fire engine I thought it was going to our house. I had read somewhere about a European royal family's having some disease which meant that if they started to bleed they never stopped; I thought I might have it too, so feared that it was curtains if I suffered the slightest cut.

I jumped four feet at a loud noise, I thought the sound of leaves in the wind was a burglar; I feared a tidal wave coming in and submerging Dublin. I was always looking at the sky edgily in case a comet was coming toward us, and on four different occasions I thought I saw the devil.

All in all I was a bag of nerves as a child, and yet I grew up into a fairly fearless, reckless adult.

But because I remember what it was like to be utterly terrified of almost everything, I am actually very sympathetic to those who think people are drilling into their homes and will come up through the floor any minute, or that they will be beaten to a pulp by the first people they meet if they are mad enough to go abroad.

How did I get the courage of a lion and stop whimpering? Well, first because of something my father once said as we looked at Smokey, the totally deranged cat, creeping around stalking an autumn leaf that was frightening him to death.

My father said it was natural for all animals, including humans, to have this sense of fear. Otherwise, he explained, we'd walk into the most desperate situations and wouldn't survive, and that's why our hearts start to race and our breathing begins to get fast, and this is called a state of "fight or flight." I found that this explanation helped me a lot, especially since I had recently been having a bit of a problem with shadows on a bus shelter that I was fairly sure were escaped gorillas.

I checked it out with my mother. She had been a nurse and was always more graphic about things than other people. She said that when we were frightened every pore in the body opened and let out gallons of sweat. The thinking was that if we were all sweaty, it made us difficult to be grabbed by anything that was pursuing us, if anything was, which it usually wasn't.

She said that this was the reason our hair stood on end, too; it was more difficult to pick up and walk off with something bristling, I supposed. We agreed that it probably wasn't as useful a response nowadays, when humans weren't covered from head to toe with hair as they used to be. Still, the principle was the same, and the old nervous system hadn't quite understood or caught up with how things had changed.

I realized there weren't any gorillas behind the bus shelter. The reason I was so afraid wasn't that I was a coward at all, it was only years of heart-racing and pore-sweating and hair-going-bolt-upright.

So I got cured. It also helped that I realized I couldn't have a good time in life if I was going to be afraid of everything, and I was mad to have a good time.

Not everyone is fortunate enough to receive such enlightenment at the age of fourteen, but it can work at any age.

And the facts are all correct. I checked it out for you recently in a biology book. It wasn't as clearly explained as here, of course; a lot of stuff about the autonomic nervous system. But the bottom line is that though it's normal to feel afraid, almost all of the time there are no gorillas or snakes or personal appearances of Lucifer. There is only the poor old overreacting system that hasn't quite worked it out yet.

## THE NERVES OF YOU

Your body has forty-five miles of nerves.

# Going Up in Smoke

You can be very sure that if you go into the hospital and admit to smoking there will be a lot of heavy throat-clearing and they will tell you that almost everything that's wrong with you is caused or exacerbated by the cigarettes you keep putting into your mouth.

So before you go to the hospital maybe you should do a little research on how to kick the habit. In fact, there are some data to show that reading other people's stories of renunciation actually paves the way. Here's mine.

I got through school and college without smoking. And this was despite growing up in a home where most of those around me were wheezing and inhaling and gasping and either complaining about the cost of cigarettes if they were old enough to buy them or unraveling butts in ashtrays if they weren't.

My friends all smoked, and they never once congratulated me on my strength. They just said Maeve was useless because she never had *five* zipped away in the back of a bag like other nicer people did. I had nothing to offer in a crisis and no way of

being calmed down myself by others if the crisis was in my court.

And then one fateful day a particularly horrible acquaintance inhaled through her slim body right down to her tiny feet and told me I was very brave not to smoke. Brave? Yes. Apparently because if I had been smoking, I wouldn't have been eating a warm almond bun covered with butter.

I looked around the group. They were frighteningly elegant. They even made smoke rings, some of them. None of them had fingers covered in butter; none of their eyes were looking at the last almond bun on the plate.

We had all been to a film where Humphrey Bogart and Lauren or Ingrid or some other non-almond-bun-eating person had looked just terrific. Though I was a grown-up, sensible woman of twenty-two, earning my own living, not a preteen racked with insecurity, I can still hear myself saying to that horrible acquaintance that I'd give it a try.

That was in 1962. For the next sixteen years nobody saw me much, because I was behind a thick wall of smoke. I suppose I didn't eat as many almond buns as I had, but it didn't really matter since I was hardly visible.

I discovered interesting things, like you could

ask a total stranger for a cigarette, which you didn't normally do for a chocolate biscuit, and you couldn't really sleep well if there wasn't a pack beside you.

I wasn't very elegant. I never learned to make smoke rings. There was a lot of ash on my chest and little burns in my tights, and I was forever making loud, unpleasant throat-clearing sounds. I fell into habits I had once found disgusting in others, such as crushing butts out in the empty grapefruit rinds on breakfast plates.

But what the hell. I was a smoker, and all that sort of thing comes with the territory.

And then, in 1978, there was a bad flu in England. As I lay in bed with a pain in my chest, red-eyed and very self-pitying, I heard a newscaster on the radio say in tones both doom-laden and urgent that all over the country, the flu had turned to pneumonia in heavy smokers.

Panic-stricken, I leaped from the bed and ran to the doctor.

The waiting room was so full, patients were standing in lines around the wall, all of us spluttering and clutching our chests. When my turn came, the doctor looked up wearily. It had been a long morning.

He tried to put some sympathy into his greeting

to what may have been the ninetieth person who had sneezed on top of him in the last two hours.

"Flu?" he suggested.

"Pneumonia," I corrected. "It's pneumonia—I heard it on the radio."

Doctors often get patients who have heard

messages from the radio or outer space. They are time-consuming people. He looked at me sadly.

"Oh dear," he said.

I was desperate at this stage. "Doctor," I implored, "I would be the last person to think of mentioning the British Medical Council, but are you or are you not going to listen to my chest?"

In the background, the 150 or so meek and obedient people, who would have readily accepted that they had the flu, barked like poor sick seals in the waiting room. To humor me, and mainly to get rid of me, he took out his stethoscope and plonked it in the area of my lungs.

"Breathe in," he said through clenched teeth.

I did, and the pain was desperate.

"What do you hear?" I croaked.

"I hear that you are fat, you are forty, and you smoke five packs of cigarettes a day," he said as he wrote a prescription for antibiotics to deal with postflu infections.

He was three years on the wrong side of my age, of course, which was fairly offensive. But he was otherwise right.

"You mean the pain has to do with smoking?" I asked in disbelief.

"Oh yes, indeed," he said, and rang the bell for the next patient.

And just because it was all so obvious to him, and because he didn't even try to make me give them up, some kind of scales fell from my poor red eyes, and to this day I have never smoked another cigarette.

# Age-Old Elixirs

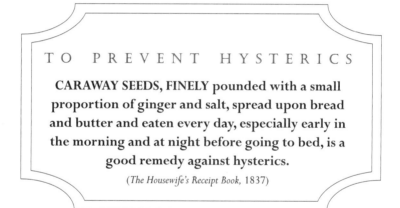

### TO PREVENT HYSTERICS

**CARAWAY SEEDS, FINELY** pounded with a small
proportion of ginger and salt, spread upon bread
and butter and eaten every day, especially early in
the morning and at night before going to bed, is a
good remedy against hysterics.

*(The Housewife's Receipt Book,* 1837)

# The Demon Rum

You will not be surprised to learn that they're not very enthusiastic about alcohol in hospitals, so be prepared for dark frowns if the subject comes up.

If you have been contemplating cutting down or even giving it up, then a trip to the hospital could be just what you need to start you off. Meanwhile, an inspiring story and some very helpful facts.

# How I Gave Up Drinking: An Inspiring Story

I had a great plan. I would drink one day a month. Every single month there would be an "Evening with Wine." I would plan this carefully for about thirty days.

And I did. The actual outings themselves were fairly spectacular because they were so eagerly anticipated.

In January I went to an Italian restaurant on my wedding anniversary and after two glasses of wine became helpless and incapable with drink and tears. I sobbed to the whole clientele, and eventually the kitchen staff, who came out to find out what was happening, how very very happy I was. I apparently listed all the shortcomings of the people I hadn't married. It took three days to get over that.

In February I had one glass of a very full-bodied red wine in South Africa and more or less passed out before being assisted to a taxi.

In March I unwisely drank some champagne on a flight to Chicago and fought bitterly with the air stewardess, who was going to marry a man she didn't love. I was so depressed by her attitude toward things that later that night I brooded too much about it and fell out of bed, breaking my nose and my toe.

In April I was so ashamed of what had happened in March I had no Evening with Wine at all.

In May it was my birthday so I had an Evening with Wine surrounded by cushions and rugs in case I fell.

And then in June I had lost the weight and I got the new hip.

Now I know all this sounds very drastic and possibly not at all helpful to normal people. But  there just might be a few extreme folks looking at this book who will be helped, which is why I decided to share my inspiring if somewhat overly dramatic tale.

I have an Evening with Wine once a week now, which isn't nearly as nice as an Evening with Wine every night. But it's four times better than once a month.

# Ten Wonderful Things About Giving Up Drink

1. You feel heroic.

2. Your liver turns nice and pink again.

3. You won't have to explain—only the worst kind of boors beg you to "have just one" these days. Actually people rarely notice if you're drinking or not. Trust me on this; it surprised me, too.

4. You don't have hangovers.

5. You save money.

6. You remember what happened.

7. You get more work done.

8. You won't find it nearly as bad as you think. Anticipating a dry evening is much worse than actually having one, and no wine is easier than a little wine. Trust me on this, too.

9. You don't get that sudden urge to eat everything that's on the table.

10. You have a load of great help out there if this advice isn't quite enough for you.

# Where Things Are

I used to think the kidneys were somewhere in the underwear area. But they're not. They are just below your bra strap, if you are of the sex and shape that wears a bra. If not, you will know where I mean.

Get a map of arteries. They look like an amazing underground rail system. We might clog them a bit less if we knew what they looked like. Be courageous and look at a picture of the large intestine and the small one. If we expect medical people to take all our parts in their stride, why should we be squeamish about how they look?

Examine a picture of a skeleton and see whether the knee bone is actually connected to the thigh bone or if it's only that way in the song.

X RAY

If a real medical text on all this is too much for you, get a child's book on the body. The basics are there, but presented much more cheerfully.

And why not take a mirror and do some investigating of your own. You look into totally unimportant things like other people's windows, open handbags, or shopping carts in a supermarket. You won't tremble nearly so much about an ear, nose, throat, or indeed any other aperture if you have examined it in good health.

## A I R - C O N D I T I O N I N G

Your nose is busy cleaning, warming, and humidifying more than 500 cubic feet of air each day.

## H I G H   W I N D

A sneeze can travel as fast as 100 miles per hour.

# Sometimes a Chest Pain Is Just a Chest Pain

Before you leap to all kinds of conclusions about a pain here or there, consider this story about the infamous chest pain.

I once went to a women journalists' conference in Central America where so much went wrong and the stress was so high that if there had been an Intensive Care Unit within miles I think all six hundred participants would have been in it.

The hotel booking system was so bad we slept three to a room, and one of my roommates woke in the night with terrible chest pains. One of the waitresses at the hotel was a third-year medical student, and since she was all we had, she stood there in her nightie while frightened women speaking various languages tried to interpret for one another by candlelight, since the generator had gone again.

I hope that by now that young girl who reassured everyone in sight is an acclaimed heart specialist in her own land. She stood there in the candlelight telling us that it need not be what we all feared.

"You see, the chest, she ees a beeg complex structure. The chest, she has many major organs besides the heart; the pain could be in any of these. She has the ribs, and they could be cracked like firewood. The chest, she has the muscles, and these could be strained by too much sex or climbing around the ruins. The chest ees also the area where unwisely chosen food could cause the indigestion."

A little color was coming back to the face of

our roommate. The banquet we had been to that night had offered a rather leathery sausage. "Please," we all silently prayed, "may this be the problem."

But the waitress was not finished. "The chest, she ees so interesting. She could hold the pleurisy, the bronchitis. . . ." She beamed with all the things the chest could hold that might not be a fatal heart attack.

Now, decades later, women from forty countries can remember her calm round face, her lack of fear, her insistence that we not choose the worst-case scenario. Not only was she right then but I imagine she has been right for all of us who have ever had a chest pain, or any pain for that matter, and been able to call up her wonderful, calming words: "The chest, she ees a beeg complex structure."

# PART 2

# At the Hospital

# You and Your Doctor

Remember the doctors are all on your side. If you
want to get better, have nothing to hide.

The doctors have heard every story before—
They will not keel over, and show you the door.

When asked do you drink, then you must not be
shy—Admit that you'd drink any harbor quite dry.

If they ask about cigarettes, don't make a joke,
Don't say "a few puffs," if it's fifty you smoke.

Doctors are often obsessed about diet.
If you eat like a glutton, then don't keep it quiet.

But tell the bad news about chocolate and fries—
It's not going to come as a total surprise.

If you think you'll forget the things that they tell,
Try writing them down in a notebook as well.

Doctors can't be clairvoyants, you have to explain
Just where you are feeling the ache or the pain.

Say which tablets you're on, and if you are able
Bring in the right bottle, its name on the label.

Though their writing is hopeless, they're really
quite kind—They're doing their best the solutions
to find.

# Things You Can Say to Annoy the Patient in the Next Bed

1. "Oh, was that your husband? I thought it was your son."

2. "Very wise of you not to have too many visitors."

3. "Will they be bringing you a proper dressing gown at all?"

4. "Would you like this book someone gave me? It's pure rubbish. I can't bear it myself."

5. "You were talking in your sleep last night; I hope you don't talk like that when you're at home with your wife!"

6. "Have you thought of getting treatment for snoring?"

7. "Would you like to see my operation scar?"

8. "Shall we all get out of bed and take a group photograph?"

9. "I was looking at your chart. I imagine you'll be here for some time."

10. "Let me tell you five jokes you might enjoy."

# Utterances From a Hospital Bed That Will Ensure You Get No More Visits

"I thought you were never going to get here."

"Oh, it's you again, is it?"

"Well, how do you *think* I am stuck in here?"

"Not more fruit—I'll turn into an orange at this rate."

"I hope you're keeping the place properly at home."

"I've read that you can take it home with you."

"They say I'm getting better, but what do they know."

"It's easy for you—you can walk away on your own two good legs."

"You'll never guess what my last visitor brought me. . . ."

"You can go now if you want to."

"You mean you're going already?"

# Ten Gifts to Suggest When Asked "What Can I Bring You?"

1.  A dozen stamped postcards to write short thank-you notes or accounts of your ailments to the outside world.

2.  A laptop tray—a thing with a flat top and a beanbag bottom—that doesn't slide off the bed.

3.  An artificial silk flower that won't eat the oxygen, need any water, annoy the nurses, or die and upset everyone.

4. A bar of ludicrously expensive designer soap that no one would ever buy in real life.

5. The loan of a Walkman or tape recorder and three talking books.

6. A bottle of really good salad dressing or vinaigrette. Hospital food can be very bland; this can spice up almost everything but the semolina.

7.  Gossipy and silly magazines. Energetic sporting, mountaineering, or boxing publications can make the weak feel weaker still.

8.  For women: A pinkish scarf to drape around the shoulders is inclined to make the grayest face a bit more lively.

9.  For men: A small bottle of expensive cologne to slap around the chops and make you feel more desirable.

10.  Some vague proof in the form of a card with many signatures on it that friends, family, neighbors, or colleagues have not forgotten you.

# On the Subject of Elastic Stockings

I don't want you to think that I am being too sunny and cheerful; believe me, I can see the dark side as well as anyone else!

You may encounter elastic stockings during your stay in the hospital. Not everyone does, but if you do—mark my words—they will be about the greatest nightmare that you come across there. These are terrible things that apparently are hugely beneficial. Nobody ever tells you about them in advance, so I thought I would warn you.

## THE GOOD NEWS

They are there to stop clots that might form if your legs are allowed to roam free, and somehow they are meant to hold you together after operations, or to ease your varicose veins, which is all very admirable and much to be desired.

They don't hurt at all when they're on. In fact, they actually feel very comfortable when they're in place.

That's about it.

## THE BAD NEWS
The bad news is that putting them on and taking them off is like having a skin graft. You see someone approaching, holding this unyielding white cloth container that looks as if it wouldn't fit over your thumb, let alone over your entire leg—and you grit your teeth.

But first the stocking that is already on has to

come off. Once it does, you're afraid to look in case most of your flesh had come off with it, but amazingly your poor leg looks intact. Sad and white, but still all there.

You remember the times when you didn't have to go through

this ritual every day and you wonder why you didn't feel ludicrously carefree and happy from dawn to dusk.

It's no use suggesting, as I did, that maybe you don't need to wash your legs all that much, and that possibly you could keep the elastic stockings on for a week or so. They don't like that notion—it sounds filthy and disgusting to them.

Legs just have to be washed every day, that's it, which means you have to have the things removed and replaced daily.

I used to hate this more than anything else in the hospital. But bad as it was having the elastic stockings put on and taken off by kind, trained hospital staff, it was totally horrific trying to do it at home.

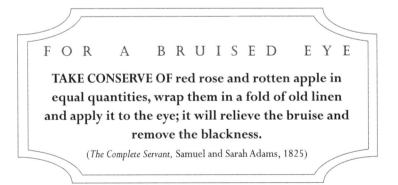

FOR A BRUISED EYE

TAKE CONSERVE OF red rose and rotten apple in equal quantities, wrap them in a fold of old linen and apply it to the eye; it will relieve the bruise and remove the blackness.

(*The Complete Servant,* Samuel and Sarah Adams, 1825)

How to pull on and take off Elastic stockings

In theory—in someone's mad theory—you are meant to be able to do it yourself. Supposedly, it's all a matter of getting the heel in the right place and then pulling the stocking up with a pick-up-stick.

Trust me: It doesn't work. You really need the services of a kind, good spouse, partner, relative, friend, or passerby—someone firm enough to refuse to let you grow fungus on your legs by allowing you some days' respite between the changes, technical enough to work out the amazing geometry of getting the heel on first, kind enough to put up with all the ungrateful yelps, optimistic enough to realize that this is unlikely to last forever, and persuasive enough to convince you that one blissful day, the authorities will allow you to let your legs run free again.

# When Kids Come to Visit

A friend of mine who was in the hospital for some months ached for the visits of her two young children.

But they were always a disaster.

They began each visit by being overwhelmed by the unfamiliar surroundings.

Then they objected to all the grown-up conversation that had to take place.

Finally they sobbed when their mother wasn't able to get out of her bed and come home with them.

She was so upset after visiting hour that the other women in her ward decided to find a solution.

They got a big scrapbook and told the children they had to do drawings of all the people in the different beds and write down their names so that their mom would know who was where.

Then they were told they had to learn the people's names and ailments so that they could keep their mother informed on what was happening.

The kids asked the nurses, doctors, interns, and volunteers to sign the book as if they were all famous celebrities.

The innocence of the children was so infectious that everyone joined in with enthusiasm.

Not everyone can create such a triumphant scene for young visitors, but if you do have children coming to see you, it's good to remember that a lot of what you as a patient accept as totally normal can seem frightening and bizarre to them.

The drip that is attached to your arm has become second nature to you, but to them it's frightening until you explain what it does and that it doesn't hurt.

The oxygen suspended over the bed might seem terrifying until you tell them how simply it works and how well it makes you feel if you really need it.

They are awkward about bandages, splints, neck braces, or anything unexpected, until you tell them what they're for.

And then, children will surprise you with the casual way they accept things.

To a child, a long-term illness is one that means a week away from school.

To a child, an accident means that a tree or a gate or a wall was in the wrong place—it doesn't mean that they may be getting feeble.

Young visitors can be the best thing that could ever happen to you, even if they're not your own. It's often possible to hijack someone else's young visitors, especially if you have a game or jigsaw puzzle or sweets very much in evidence.

Children are happy to discuss your ailments and ask things like whether you will ever walk again in a way that their more uptight elders never would.

They are delightful company and will make wonderful friends, as long as you remember the two things you must never say to any child:

"Aren't you a handsome little boy."

or

"Aren't you a lovely big girl."

# An Elegant Medicine Cupboard

For some reason people always peep into your medicine cupboard. Fool them totally. Have lovely, fresh-looking things in it, with no sign of suppositories, false-teeth fixative, violent laxatives, or unmerciful cures for diarrhea. Instead have:

—Harmless-looking vitamins

—Hangover cures to show what a racy life you lead

—Some essential oils for aromatherapy

—A small whip that will have them speculating about you for years

Put the things you really need in a different box entirely. Then cover the box with a nice towel and leave it as a little stand for the lavatory brush. Nobody will dream of investigating it.

# Six Ways to Make Yourself Pointlessly Anxious While You Are in the Hospital

1.  You must suddenly think that the entire running of your life has collapsed—so much so that the family cannot live without you. Your cats and dogs are sitting outside the house yowling at the moon waiting for you to come back.

And at work, all has disintegrated and nobody knows where anything is. This should ensure that you won't sleep for some hours.

2.  If you find that this method is not working properly, you could think of an even worse possibility. Like this one. Your home is managing just

perfectly without you, everyone's getting on with their tasks, it's all running smoothly. The cat and dog have forgotten you ever existed.

Your office is ticking along just as it did when you were there. In fact, your coworkers have to remember what exactly it was you used to do.

3.  Your family has put your house up for sale.

4.  If people don't come and see you in great droves, then you could tell yourself that you always

suspected they hated you and now you know you were right. You could lie there and look at the ceiling with great tears in your eyes, forgetting that you have been told to rest and that visits are restricted.

5.  There's an even more entertaining way of driving yourself mad on this theme. Suppose people DO

come to see you. You must tell yourself that it has nothing to do with friendship or concern. It's all because they have heard you are terminally ill or because half of them have had an affair with your spouse at some time or another and feel extremely guilty.

6.  You must examine all the members of the hospital staff very carefully. If they are young, then you must decide immediately

that they are raw and inexperienced and obviously know nothing at all. If they seem to be reasonably mature, then you must tell yourself that they are doddering and senile and far too confused to have learned any modern-day techniques.

# On the Subject of Bedpans

One of the things people hate about going to the hospital is knowing they will no longer be in control.

You have to work by someone else's timetable.

You have to obey someone else's rules.

The final indignity is the thought of not being able to go to the bathroom alone.

Fear of the bedpan is high amongst anxieties. But it often causes far more distress than it has to.

Nurses and hospital personnel say that patients make it more difficult on themselves and everyone else by being too shy.

It's only natural to be mortified/horrified that

what is usually done in the privacy of a bathroom has to be done in a container in bed and that, worse, the results have to be removed by someone else.

I made official inquiries about what was the very best thing patients could do about this attitude. And the answer was unanimous. Nurses didn't want any production over the bedpan. It was part of their work; people who couldn't move from the bed had to have them.

Politeness is always acceptable, and nurses, like everyone else, always appreciate a word of thanks. But apologies are out of place. They're attempts—idiotic ones—to deny bodily functions.

As one nurse said very succinctly to me when like everyone I apologized for having to use a bedpan: "Look at it this way, Maeve—if I weren't washing your bottom, I'd be washing someone else's." Which, indeed, was undeniable.

# "What'll It Be?"

Nothing could be more welcome than a kind friend with a thermos filled with ice and a really great nonalcoholic drink. You MIGHT even take to it so much that you will continue the practice when you get home. These are six that I would enjoy:

1.  Ice-cold ginger ale mixed with cranberry juice

2.  A root beer float

3.  A tall, cool glass of freshly squeezed orange juice

4.  Tomato juice with a little Tabasco, served with a topping of finely chopped red peppers

5. Strawberries and bananas blended together and served in a tall glass with fresh mint

6. Iced coffee in a big glass mug served with a huge scoop of ice cream on top

# Baring Your Body

Did anyone ever liken going for a medical examination to entering a beauty competition?

Yet nurses say they are driven mad by time-wasting modesty and insanely apologetic attitudes about what is, after all, just a human body. Although sympathetic and aware of how low some people's self-esteem can be, particularly at a time of ill health, medical staff say they often wish there were some kind of basic training course for patients, something to convince them this is not an exhibition or a peep show, but an attempt to find out what is wrong with them and to cure it.

They report patients who clutch on to hospital

gowns when asked to remove them as if the doctors or nurses were about to play music and have them do "the Full Monty" for the X-ray department. Many women tense up at the thought that people might be studying their stretch marks or odd stomach flaps and reporting their deeply unsatisfactory findings all over the city.

Yes, the medical examination does seem just one further indignity, inviting humiliation and vulnerability at the very moment when it's least tolerable. None of us would choose to show to complete strangers the parts of ourselves that most other human eyes don't reach.

But they have seen all those bits of people before. In fact, they are seeing such bits all day long.

When we realize that self-consciousness is self-obsessiveness, it's much easier to take off our clothes as quickly as possible and get whatever it is done.

I speak from the point of view of someone not at all satisfied with her body image, but lucky enough

to know it's of no interest to anyone on earth except myself.

I was greatly helped by accidentally visiting a nudist colony. I was going there as a journalist to write about it, and arrived on the bus with my clothes on, intending to leave them on.

But when the bus left, I was told by a staffer that unless I took my clothes off I would have to sit on the side of the road for eight hours until another bus came along. It was in Yugoslavia, and it was very hot. I took my clothes off.

I went into the place and hid behind a bush. Then I crept out a bit and sat sort of covering myself, with my handbag on my lap and my arms across my chest, smoking in a frenzy.

And then slowly I noticed that people with the most horrific shapes and dangling bits and extraordinary appendages were going by, and that nobody was paying a blind bit of notice. So I got the courage to slink along the wall toward the restaurant.

I joined the regular campers, and we sat in cafés all day with bits of us falling into the soup and our bottoms roasting undignifiedly on hot seats. Occasionally we fell into the sea without bothering to put on or take off swimming costumes. And eventually my eyes stopped looking at the white bits of people and I just got on with the day like everyone else.

It was about the most liberating thing I ever did. I would wish the same sense of freedom to all those I see covering themselves and refusing to come out from behind screens.

# PART 3

# Home Again

## Relax: Let Them Look After You

WHO SAYS THE SHOW MUST GO ON?

There really is no good reason for it. If you're ill, recovering from an illness or operation, or just not able to cope for a bit, this is the time to call in the troops.

We must all try to break the habit of a lifetime—thinking we can deal with everything—and instead decide we should allow those who are concerned about us to do something to help.

People actually LIKE to be told what they can do if they offer to help. They are always offering, begging you to think of something they can do for you at this time. Suppose you were to say to people that there really were a few things

they could do that would be a huge help to you? Aren't *you* truly delighted to do something to help someone else?

In fact, if we are brutally honest, we would all prefer to do one fairly specific thing to help, rather than to sign on for life as a slave.

So a truly thoughtful patient might just think up a list of ten little jobs to help the ten people who've offered their help. They will then be overjoyed and feel important and indispensable. You'll be doing them a favor.

You could ask someone to:

Cut the grass

Do the ironing

Take out the rubbish bins

Make you a soup

Take the dog for a walk

Vacuum the floor

Defrost the fridge

**Paint your nails**

**Go to the bookie**

**And a million other things you can think of while you rest and recover your strength.**

# Gadgets for the Wise

A lot of the aids for the disabled or the elderly advertised in catalogues and available in stores can be extraordinarily useful for those who as yet have no official need for them. It's a wise person who becomes familiar with such items ahead of the posse.

—A safety rail for the shower. You might not need it to hang on to yet, but it's very helpful when you're washing your hair and are blind as a bat.

—Those book-holder things they have for recipe

books also work splendidly for your ordinary reading.

—A piece of strong ribbon or a scarf tied to the car door handle, so that you can pull it shut without straining.

—A one-hand tray that has a kind of basket handle is terrific for going out to the garden or just upstairs.

—Long-handled shoehorns and slip-on shoes make good sense at any age.

—Velcro fastenings are a hell of a lot easier than buttons in the places that are hard to reach.

—Raised flower beds. Have them in the garden NOW, not later. You can always lean on them with a drink in your hand and do a bit of absentminded gardening.

that's not really what the pick-up-stick is meant for – DEAR!

—A "goods upward" box or basket on the bottom step saves on trips upstairs, where it becomes a "goods downward" receptacle for things that want to descend.

—A long-handled dustpan is a joyous thing. You'll wonder why they ever made the other kind.

—A pick-up-stick, a delightful tool for reaching anything from a book on a high shelf to a piece of newspaper that has blown away.

# The Eccentric Convalescent

While you are getting better, take the chance to do all kinds of things you would never have done before. It's your time, and you are entitled.

**CLOTHES**

If you want to wear a cowboy hat and everyone says that it's totally inappropriate, then you should wear it with total confidence during your recovery time.

I always wanted to wear a pink feather boa but was put off by the faces of my nearest and dearest, but while I was getting better I wore one all the time, and nobody dared to comment on it.

**RECIPES**

As you may not be able to leave the house and go out to restaurants for a bit, learn how to make at least five new dishes that you've never tried before. Ask your visitors to bring you ingredients and get on with it. A man I met in the hospital became so good at making soups that he now does them for a local restaurant, and I discovered hidden talents for Thai cooking myself, once people went shopping for lemongrass, coconut, and lime.

---

### BE A FRIEND TO YOUR FEET

One-fourth of the 206 bones in your body
are in your feet.

---

# Chain Letter for Weary Women

**SEND A CHAIN LETTER. I LOVE THIS ONE.**

Dear Friend,

This letter was started by a woman like yourself in hopes of bringing relief to other tired and discontented women. Unlike most chain letters, this one does not cost you anything.

You bundle up your husband, partner, or boyfriend and send him to the woman whose name appears at the top of this list. Then add your own name to the bottom of the list and send a copy of this letter to five of your friends who are equally tired and discontented.

When you come to the top of the list you will receive 3,125 men, and some of them are bound to be better than the one you gave up.

DO NOT BREAK THIS CHAIN. One woman did and she received her own man back.

## CATCHING UP

All the people on my corridor in the hospital vowed that when we got home we would spend no time feeling sorry for ourselves, but instead would catch up on all those things we had intended to do for years and had never got around to.

— . . . labeling the videotapes
— . . . putting CDs in alphabetical order
— . . . rewriting our address books
— . . . weeding out our photo albums
— . . . asking for a drawer a day to be brought to us so that we can spring-clean it thoroughly
— . . . going through old magazines and journals, throwing most of them out

Because I am very bossy and had taken all their names and addresses, I checked whether any of the other patients had actually carried out their resolutions, and everyone had done SOMETHING. Not as much as we'd intended, of course; we'd all done a lot of lounging around and sleeping and watching programs we did not really want to watch on television. But because we had promised, we felt we had to make some attempt. In my own case, I liberated half a room of old magazines by clipping six pages—which was all I really needed out of four hundred publications that I thought I could never throw out.

# PART 4

# Postscript

# In an Ideal World

In an ideal world every patient would be a twinkling, smiling, grateful person propped up with pillows and overcome with gratitude that we have come to visit.

The perfect patient's face would  crack open into a huge smile of delight, as if no other person on earth could possibly be as welcome as we are. There would be nice fresh fruit available, a few chocolate  truffles, maybe even books or magazines we could borrow because the patient has already read them and would be happy to have the space on the shelf cleared.

The patient would have no complaints about anything: the prognosis is good, the doctors are inspired, the nurses are angels, and the hospital food is fine.

We'd all visit the hospital happily if we could be sure the patient we were there to see was going to be like that.

But there will be days when we approach a bed and know that it's going to be far from that.

I was in a hospital ward and heard a woman greet a daughter who had just endured a horrific journey involving one train and two bus transfers. The mother's words were that she need not bother to visit again wearing that short skirt and looking like a tart.

I saw a man welcome his white-faced, anxious wife during visiting time by saying that she had yet again brought the wrong newspaper and was there a chance that one day she might get something right.

I once went to see a fairly feisty elderly woman who decided that she would rather go to sleep than talk to me. Sleep, she explained, was one of the few pleasures she had left to her and she felt a wave of it coming over her at that very moment; she was sure I understood.

I have seen a three-year-old come into a

maternity ward clutching flowers for his mother, only to find her clutching and cooing over a small, screaming red-faced baby, with no similar hugs for him. And on top of all this, he was meant to be pleased that this horrible thing had joined the family.

And in a perfect world every patient would look out of bed and see a regular stream of delightful, concerned visitors coming in carrying exactly the right gift.

These ideal visitors would want to know the most detailed minutiae of every happening since they had last visited.

They would be fascinated by any change in medication, temperature charts, or blood pressure levels.

They would beg for details of what the consultant said, what the resident identified, and whether the nurse taking blood had found a good sturdy vein.

They would remember the name of every single staff member you had mentioned.

They would bring warm personal greetings from almost everyone in the outer world and give the impression that society as we know it had almost broken down because of your temporary absence.

But, of course, that's not going to happen either. It's a far from perfect world. I must explain that I am an avid reader of self-help books; I have shelves of them at home. I truly think that almost everything can be learned from a manual. But if you have hundreds of manuals, as I do, that tell you how to flatten your stomach, have perfect skin, thrive on stress, play demon bridge, cook with yeast, put more time in your life . . . then you will realize that if you get one single piece of useful information from any manual, you are doing well.

Wendy Shea and I, hopeless but caring and cheerful patients, and well-meaning hospital visitors

in turn, hope just that there has been SOMETHING in these pages that made you believe that things aren't quite as bad as you thought
they were.

Just one little insight is all we want for you. Then it will have been well worth our while writing and illustrating this bossy book.